Jokes Old and New

Jokes Old and New

© C.R. Draper, 2020

'All rights reserved. No part of this book may be reproduced in any form or by any electronic or mechanical means, without permission in writing from the copyright owner.'

ISBN: 978-1-909986-69-5

Contents

Animal Jokes 7

Animals on Holiday 27

Bird Jokes. 29

Cat Jokes 34

Books, Films and TV 36

Christmas Jokes. 39

Circus Jokes 42

Crime 44

Diet Jokes. 47

Dinosaur Jokes 49

Doctors and Dentist 51

Farts 59

Food and Cooking 61

Friends and Family 72

Geography. 76

Ghost Jokes. 80

History Jokes 83

Jokes 87

Lightbulb Jokes 91

Magic Jokes 98

Marriage and Relationship Jokes. 99

Maths Jokes 105

Miscellaneous Jokes 111

Money 118

Monsters, dragons and other fictitious creatures. . 119

Mummy Jokes 122

Music Jokes 124

Planes, Trains and Automobiles · · · · · · · · · · · · · · · · 129

Presents and birthdays 131

Professions. 132

Pub 138

Retail. 140

Riddles 143

School Jokes	149
Science Jokes	153
Skeleton Jokes	165
Space	167
Star Wars	169
Time	174
Technology	176
Water	178
What do you call?	181
What do you get if you cross?	187
Winter Jokes	190
Words	193

Animal Jokes

What do wolves say to each other?

Howl's it going?

What do you get from a clever oyster?

Pearls of wisdom.

What's the difference between a weasel and a stoat?

A weasel is weasily recognised and a stoat is stoatily different.

What's a dog's favourite spice?

Pup-rika.

The Alphabet is terrifying.
A bee sea? No thank you.

⸺

How did the puppy stop the DVD?
He used paws.

⸺

What did the doe say when she was worried?
Oh deer.

⸺

Why do cows have hooves?
Because they lactose.

⸺

Why can't a leopard hide?
They're always spotted.

⸺

When is a dog not a dog?
When it is pure bread.

⸺

Why are dogs such bad dancers?
They have two left feet.

What do you get when you cross a cocker spaniel, a poodle and a rooster?

A cocklepoodledoo.

What type of dog can tell the time?

A watchdog.

What happened to the hyena who accidently swallowed an oxo cube?

He became a laughing stock.

Why was the rabbit arrested?

He was charged with Hare-assment!

Where do rabbits go after they're married?

On their bunnymoon.

How can you tell that carrots help you see in the dark?

Have you ever seen a rabbit with a torch?

What do you get if you pour boiling water down a rabbit hole?

A hot cross bunny.

What's worse that finding a worm in your apple?
Finding half a worm in your apple.

What do whales eat for dinner?
Fish and ships.

"Where do fish keep their money?'
In riverbanks

Why didn't the prawn share its afternoon tea?
It was a little shellfish.

What do you give a deaf fish?
A herring aid.

How do cod and mackerel watch the news?
On the telefishon.

What do you call twenty rabbits walking backwards?
A receding hareline!

What happens to cows during an earthquake?
They give milk shakes!

What do you get if you sit under a cow?
A pat on the head.

What did Mama cow say to Baby cow?
It's pasture bedtime.

What do you get if an elephant sits on your friend?
A flat-mate.

What's an elephant's favourite game?
Squash.

What do you call a cow eating grass in a paddock?
A lawn mooer.

What do you call a cow with no milk?
An udder failure.

What do you call a sleeping bull?
A bull-dozer.

What do you call a grumpy cow?
Moo-dy.

What party games do cows like best?
Moosical chairs.

Why do cows lie down when it's cold?
To keep each udder warm.

What do you call an explosive monkey?
A baboom.

Did you hear about the crocodile with the camera?
He was snap-happy.

Why are some fish at the bottom of the ocean?
Because they dropped out of school!

Why don't ants get sick?

Because they have little anty-bodies.

Why did the man give the pony some water?

It was a little hoarse.

What type of horses only go out at night?

Nightmares.

What do you call a horse that lives next door?

A neigh-bour.

Why did the pony cough?

He was a little hoarse.

What did the pony say when it had a sore throat?

I'm a little hoarse.

What do you call a pony that likes needlework and pottery?

A hobby horse.

Why are elephants so poor?

Because they work for peanuts.

What does a doctor give an elephant who's going to be sick?

Plenty of room.

How do you get down off an elephant?

You don't, you get down off a duck.

Why did the monkey like the banana?

Because it had appeal.

Why don't monkeys play cards in the jungle?

There are too many cheetahs there.

How do monkeys get down the stairs?

They slide down the banana-ster!

How does a monkey make toast?

Under a gorilla.

Which animal was out of bounds?

The exhausted kangaroo.

What to polar bears eat for lunch?

Ice berg-ers.

What do you call a grizzly bear caught in the rain?

A drizzly bear.

What's black and white, black and white, and black and white?

A panda bear rolling down a hill.

What is black and white and red all over?

A panda bear with a sunburn.

Where do insects do their shopping?

In a flea market.

What's the healthiest type of insect?

The vitamin bee.

What was the insect's favourite sport?
Cricket.

Why did the bees have sticky hair?
Because they used a honeycomb.

Why didn't the butterfly go to the dance?
Because it was a moth ball.

Two silk worms were in a race. Who won?
It was a tie.

Where does the biggest ever spider live?
On the world wide web.

What's worse than raining cats and dogs?
Hailing taxis.

Did you hear about the cat who sucked a lemon?
He was a sourpuss.

What kind of cats like to go bowling?

Alley cats.

What is a cat's favourite colour?

Purr-ple.

What is a cat's favourite song?

Three Blind Mice.

What do cats like to watch on television?

The evening mews.

What did the cat have for breakfast?

Mice Crispies.

Why do mice need oiling?

Because they squeak.

What is a cat's favourite game?

Mewsical chairs.

What does a cat rest it's head on at night?
A caterpillow.

What is the strongest creature in the sea?
A mussel.

Where do fish sleep?
On the seabed.

What do fish and maps have in common?
They both have scales.

Where do sharks come from?
Finland.

What is a frog's favourite year?
Leap year.

What is a frog's favourite game?
Leapfrog.

What is a frog's favourite game?
Croak-et.

What is a frog's favourite flower?
Croak-us.

What is a frog's favourite cold drink?
Croak-a-cola.

What is a frog's favourite hot drink?
Hot croak-o.

What is a frog's favourite music?
Hip hop.

How did the toad die?
It croaked.

Why was the glow worm disappointed?
Because her children weren't very bright.

What's green, cold blooded and follows the yellow brick road?

The lizard of Oz

⁂

What do you call a snake that travels around on the front of a car?

A windscreen viper.

⁂

What do you call a snake who works for the government?

A civil serpent.

⁂

Why is there no point playing jokes on snakes?

You can't pull their legs.

⁂

What's a snake's favourite subject?

Hisssstory

⁂

What did the buffalo say to his son when he went away on a trip?

Bi-son.

What is a sheep's favourite game?

Baa-dminton.

What do sheep do on a Summer evening?

Have a baa- baa-que.

What happened when the sheep pen broke?

The sheep had to use a pencil.

What did one polite sheep say to the other sheep?

After ewe.

What animals are on legal documents?

Seals.

How do you close a letter under the sea?

With a seal.

How do two snails fight?

They slug it out.

What did the snail call his home?

Michelle.

⁎⁎⁎⁎⁎⁎⁎⁎⁎⁎⁎⁎⁎

A Snail without a shell should move a bit faster.

But it's actually more sluggish.

⁎⁎⁎⁎⁎⁎⁎⁎⁎⁎⁎⁎⁎

How many skunks does it take to stink up a house?

A phew.

⁎⁎⁎⁎⁎⁎⁎⁎⁎⁎⁎⁎⁎

What did the judge say when the skunk walked into the courtroom?

Odour in the court.

⁎⁎⁎⁎⁎⁎⁎⁎⁎⁎⁎⁎⁎

What do you call an alligator detective?

An investi-gator.

⁎⁎⁎⁎⁎⁎⁎⁎⁎⁎⁎⁎⁎

What's a pig's favourite ballet?

Swine lake.

⁎⁎⁎⁎⁎⁎⁎⁎⁎⁎⁎⁎⁎

What did the pig say when the farmer grabbed his tail?

That's the end of me.

Why did the pig run away from the pigsty?

He felt that the other pigs were taking him for grunted.

What happened when a tortoise collided with a terrapin?

It was a turtle disaster.

Why did the boy say his pet was called tiny?

He said it was, "because he's my newt."

How do you stop a hippo from charging?

Take away its credit cards.

When do squirrels say, "woof, woof"?

When they eat acorns and bark.

What's red and black and red and black?

A zebra with sunburn.

What do you feed an invisible cat?

Evaporated milk.

What do you call a sad fish?

A frownder.

What do you call a beehive that has no exits?

Un-bee-lievable.

What do you call an annoyed lobster?

A frustacean.

What's the difference between a coyote and a flea?

One howls on the prairie while the other prowls on the hairy.

Where do lizards go to fix their fallen tails?

The retail shop.

Where did Noah keep a record of his bees?

In the Ark hives.

I went into a pet shop and asked for twelve bees. The shopkeeper counted out thirteen and handed them over.

"You've given me one too many."

"That one is a freebie."

⁂

Did you heard about the monkeys who shared an Amazon account?

They were prime mates.

⁂

What do you call a bacterial disease caused by two grizzlies ?

Twobearculosis.

⁂

Bear walks into a bar and says to the bartender: "One whiskey and .... one coke.

"Why the big pause?" asks the bartender.

"I don't know, I was born with them," says the bear.

⁂

Why did the lion cross the road?

To stop the zebra crossing.

Some small aquatic mammals have escaped from the Zoo.

Otter chaos.

⁂

My pet rodent doesn't have a name.

He's anonymouse.

⁂

If a pig loses its voice, is it disgruntled?

⁂

Why do male ants float in water ?

Because they are boy-ant.

⁂

I was walking in the jungle and saw a lizard on his hind legs telling jokes. I turned to a local tribesman and said "That lizards really funny!"

The tribesman replied, "That's not a lizard...

He's a stand up chameleon..."

⁂

Animals on Holiday

Did you hear about the sheep that went on holiday?
They went to Baa-bados

Did you hear about the birds that went on holiday?
They went to the Canary Islands.

Why do birds fly South in winter?
It's too far to walk.

Why did the owl say, "Tweet, tweet?"
Because she didn't give a hoot.

Did you hear about the lions that went on holiday?
It was a catastrophe.

How do chickens get out of their shells?
They eggs-it them.

Did you hear about the chickens that went on holiday?
There was foul play but they had an eggcellent time.

Did you hear about the forest holiday?
There was a lot of monkeying about.

What noise does an exploding monkey make?
BaBOON.

Did you hear about the ocean holiday?
They had a whale of a time.

Bird Jokes

Why do sea-gulls fly over the sea?

Because if they flew over the bay they would be bagels!

What do you call a crate of ducks?

A box of quackers.

What happened when the duck went to the comedy show?

He quacked up.

How can you find a chicken?

Eggs marks the spot.

What happened when the chicken misbehaved at school?

He was eggspelled.

Why was the chicken rubbing her head?

Because she had an eggache.

What did the chicken say when it laid a square egg?

Owwww.

What do you call a duck that just doesn't fit in?

Mallardjusted.

Why does a chicken coop only have two doors?

Because if it had four, it would be a chicken sedan.

What time do ducks wake up?

At the quack of dawn.

Why does a flamingo stand on one leg?

Because if he lifted that leg off the ground he would fall down.

Did you hear the story about the peacock?
Yes, it's a beautiful tale.

What is even smarter than a talking bird?
A spelling bee.

Why do hummingbirds hum?
Because they forget the words.

What do you give a sick bird?
Tweetment.

Two birds were sitting on a perch.
One said to the other, "it smells of fish."

What do birds eat for breakfast?
Tweetabix.

What flies through the jungle, singing opera?
The Parrots of Penzance.

Why do pet shops always sell out of birds before any other animal?

They go cheep.

What's the difference between a fly and a bird?

A bird can fly but a fly can't bird.

What bird is always out of breath?

A puffin.

Why did the lark use a pair of hair tongs on her tail feathers?

She thought it was the curly bird who gets the worm.

Why were the geese overweight?

They couldn't stop gobbling.

Which sea bird can dance?

A pelican-can.

My friend blocked me on Facebook because I post too many bird puns.

Well, toucan play at that game.

⁕⁕⁕⁕⁕⁕⁕⁕⁕⁕⁕⁕

I just grilled a chicken.

But it still wouldn't tell me why it crossed the road.

⁕⁕⁕⁕⁕⁕⁕⁕⁕⁕⁕⁕

My pet chicken tells the best egg jokes.

She is a top comedi~hen.

⁕⁕⁕⁕⁕⁕⁕⁕⁕⁕⁕⁕

Did you know that male owls can't try to gain the love or affection of a female owl in the rain.

They say it's too wet to woo.

⁕⁕⁕⁕⁕⁕⁕⁕⁕⁕⁕⁕

One bird can't finish an entire bowl of Fruit Loops,

but Toucan.

⁕⁕⁕⁕⁕⁕⁕⁕⁕⁕⁕⁕

Cat Jokes

Cat puns freak meowt.

Seriously, I'm not kitten.

If the Earth was flat, cats would push everything off it.

If cats could text you back, they wouldn't.

Don't tell me what to do, you are not my cat.

Cats spend half their life asleep and half making viral videos.

I dressed my dog as a cat.

Now he won't come when I call him.

Petting a cat will leave you feline good.

Live long and pawsper.

What should you do when your cats not feline well.

Call a purramedic.

Why does your cat sit on your laptop?

She's helping you purrcrastinate.

What is a cat's favourite colour?

Purrple.

What do you call a pile of cats?

A meowtain.

Dogs can't operate MRI scanners, but catscan.

Dogs can order lab tests though.

Letting the cat out of the bag, is easier than putting it back in.

Books, Films and TV

A man went into a library and asked "Do you have any books on shelving?"

The librarian said, "Yes, all of them".

Just read a book about the history of glue.

Couldn't put it down.

My book on clocks finally arrived.

It's about time!

My wife: "Why don't you stop telling terrible Dad jokes and write a book instead?"

Me: "That's…… a novel idea."

I just watched a program about beavers.

Best dam program I ever saw.

⁎⁎⁎⁎⁎⁎⁎⁎⁎⁎⁎⁎⁎

I'm making a new documentary on how to fly a plane.

We're currently filming the pilot.

⁎⁎⁎⁎⁎⁎⁎⁎⁎⁎⁎⁎⁎

I've just written a book about falling down a staircase.

It's a step by step guide.

⁎⁎⁎⁎⁎⁎⁎⁎⁎⁎⁎⁎⁎

People say I'm a plagiarist.

Their words, not mine.

⁎⁎⁎⁎⁎⁎⁎⁎⁎⁎⁎⁎⁎

What kind of magazines do cows read?

Cattlelogs.

⁎⁎⁎⁎⁎⁎⁎⁎⁎⁎⁎⁎⁎

Just been reading a fantastic new book all about the life of a short ballerina.

It called, 'The girl with the dragging tutu'.

⁎⁎⁎⁎⁎⁎⁎⁎⁎⁎⁎⁎⁎

Breaking : Archaeologists believe that they've uncovered a cache of pencils that belonged to Shakespeare.

A spokesperson for the dig said they're so badly chewed on the ends. We can't tell if they're 2B or not 2B.

⁎⁎⁎⁎⁎⁎⁎⁎⁎⁎⁎⁎⁎

I took the wife to an Indian restaurant last night.

We ordered from the 'C.S Lewis set menu'.

It's like the normal menu only naanier.

⁎⁎⁎⁎⁎⁎⁎⁎⁎⁎⁎⁎⁎

A lion and a witch were carrying a wardrobe down the street..

I said 'where are you going with that?'

'Narnia business'

⁎⁎⁎⁎⁎⁎⁎⁎⁎⁎⁎⁎⁎

I've been reading a book about anti-gravity, I can't put it down!

⁎⁎⁎⁎⁎⁎⁎⁎⁎⁎⁎⁎⁎

Yesterday, I watched a documentary on the history of the WD-40.

It was non friction.

⁎⁎⁎⁎⁎⁎⁎⁎⁎⁎⁎⁎⁎

Christmas Jokes

Why shouldn't you eat Christmas decorations?

You might get tinsillitis.

What did one angel say to the other angel?

Halo there.

What did the salt say to the pepper on Christmas morning?

Seasonings greetings.

What's different about the alphabet at Christmas?

It has no 'L'.

Doctor, I'm afraid I've got a mince pie stuck in my ear.

I can put some cream on it.

⁌⁌⁌⁌⁌⁌⁌⁌⁌⁌⁌⁌

What's the difference between St George and one of Santa's reindeer?

One slays a dragon and the other's draggin' a sleigh.

⁌⁌⁌⁌⁌⁌⁌⁌⁌⁌⁌⁌

Why can't Christmas trees knit?

They keep dropping their needles.

⁌⁌⁌⁌⁌⁌⁌⁌⁌⁌⁌⁌

What did Father Christmas say to Mrs Christmas when he looked out the window?

Looks like rain dear.

⁌⁌⁌⁌⁌⁌⁌⁌⁌⁌⁌⁌

How do you show your appreciation for Father Christmas?

Sant-applause.

⁌⁌⁌⁌⁌⁌⁌⁌⁌⁌⁌⁌

What do reindeers use to decorate their antlers?

Horn-aments.

⁌⁌⁌⁌⁌⁌⁌⁌⁌⁌⁌⁌

Who holds all Santa's books for him?

The books-elf.

Who is always following the first eleven elves?
The tw-elf.

Who is the smelliest elf?
Stinkerbell.

What do elves learn at school?
The elf-abet.

Why did the elves photos look rubbish?
They were all pixie-lated.

What should you feed an elf who wants to be taller?
'elf raising flour.

What do elves make sandwiches with?
Shortbread.

There was once a famous Viking called Rudolph the Red. One day, he looked outside and asked his wife to bring the washing in because it looked like it was going to be a wet day. His wife asked, "what makes you say that?" The Viking replied, "Rudolph the Red knows rain, dear."

Circus Jokes

Why won't cannibals eat clowns?

Because they taste funny.

What happened when the short fortune-teller who escaped from prison?

She was a small medium at large.

Why material do you use to make a clown outfit?

Poly-jester.

A clown held a door open for me the other day.

I thought, "What a nice jester".

Why are circus clowns often stressed?

Because their job is "in tents".

Did you hear about the human cannonball?

He got fired!

Why did the clown go to the doctor?

Because he was feeling a little funny!

Why did the clown cross the road?

To get his rubber chicken.

What should you do if you're attacked by a group of circus performers?

Go for the juggler.

Why did the clown wear loud socks?

So his feet wouldn't fall asleep.

Why did the circus find it difficult to replace the clown that retired?

They were big shoes to fill.

Crime

As suspected, someone has been adding soil to my garden.

The plot thickens.

⁃ ✺✺✺✺✺✺✺✺✺✺✺ ⁃

I was kidnapped by a gang of mimes.

They threatened to do unspeakable things.

⁃ ✺✺✺✺✺✺✺✺✺✺✺ ⁃

Why did the thief have a nice bubble-bath before robbing the bank?

He wanted to make a clean getaway.

⁃ ✺✺✺✺✺✺✺✺✺✺✺ ⁃

Did you hear about the jewel thief who opened a shop?

He used a crowbar.

⁃ ✺✺✺✺✺✺✺✺✺✺✺ ⁃

What do you get if you dip convicts into quick-drying cement?

Hardened criminals.

I was robbed by six dwarves today.

Not happy.

A giant fly has attacked the local police...

Police have called the SWAT team.

I was attacked by 1, 3, 5, 7 and 9.

The odds were against me.

A group of leprechauns was recently busted for selling fake granite

Yeah, they were sham rocks.

Why were the two prisoners good at grammar?

Because they were always thinking about their sentences.

A man entered his home and discovered that someone had stolen every single lamp present in the house.

He was absolutely delighted.

I can't believe I got arrested for impersonating a politician.

I was just sitting around doing nothing.

Police have arrested the World tongue-twister Champion.

They said he'll be given a tough sentence.

Diet Jokes

D.I.E.T. = Did I Eat That?

D.I.E.T. = Do I Eat Today?

D.I.E.T. = Don't Indulge Every Time.

Why shouldn't you fall in love with a pastry chef?
He'll dessert you.

Did you hear about the hungry clock?
He went back four seconds.

A successful diet is the triumph of mind over platter.

I decided that becoming a vegetarian was a missed steak.

⁎⁎⁎⁎⁎⁎⁎⁎⁎⁎⁎⁎

Why should you go to the paint store if you're on a diet?

You can get thinner there.

⁎⁎⁎⁎⁎⁎⁎⁎⁎⁎⁎⁎

My mate says I'm getting fat, but in my defence.

I've had a lot on my plate recently.

⁎⁎⁎⁎⁎⁎⁎⁎⁎⁎⁎⁎

I'm on a seafood diet.

If I see food, I eat it.

⁎⁎⁎⁎⁎⁎⁎⁎⁎⁎⁎⁎

Dinosaur Jokes

Why did the pterodactyl cross the road?

Because the chicken didn't exist yet.

What do you get if you cross a dinosaur with a tea party?

A tyranosaucer.

What do you call a dinosaur that never gives up?

A try-try-try-ceratops.

What do you call a dinosaur wearing a blindfold?

Doyouthinkhesaurus.

What do you get when a dinosaur sneezes?
Out of the way.

What do you get when dinosaurs crash their cars?
Tyrannosaurus wrecks.

What do you call a dinosaur fart?
A blast from the past.

What do you call an ugly dinosaur?
An eyesaur.

Doctor and dentist

Why did the orange go to the doctor?

It wasn't peeling well.

What do you give a sick bird?

Tweetment.

What do you give a sick pig?

OINKment!

Why did the birthday cake go to the doctor?

Because it was feeling crumby!

A man goes to the Doctor and says 'I feel like a pair of curtains'

The Doctor says 'pull yourself together.'

Doctor Doctor I feel like a pack of cards.

Sit there and I'll deal with you later.

Doctor, doctor, I feel like a dog.

Sit.

Doctor, doctor I think I'm a clock.

Don't get wound up about it.

There's no need for alarm.

Doctor, doctor, I feel like a box of cheesy biscuits.

You're crackers.

Doctor, doctor, I feel like a snooker ball.

Go to the end of the queue.

Doctor doctor I think I'm invisible.

I'm sorry, I can't see you now.

Doctor, doctor I feel like a needle.
Yes, I can see your point.

✻✻✻✻✻✻✻✻✻✻✻✻✻

Doctor doctor, I feel like an apple.
We must get to the core of this.

✻✻✻✻✻✻✻✻✻✻✻✻✻

Doctor, doctor I keep thinking I'm a bell.
Leave it a week and if you're no better, give me a ring.

✻✻✻✻✻✻✻✻✻✻✻✻✻

Doctor, doctor, I think I'm a wastepaper bin.
Don't talk rubbish.

✻✻✻✻✻✻✻✻✻✻✻✻✻

Doctor, doctor, I think I'm a bridge.
What's come over you.
Two cyclists, five cars, three trucks and a double-decker bus.

✻✻✻✻✻✻✻✻✻✻✻✻✻

Doctor, doctor, I keep thinking I'm a plant.
We need to get to the root of this problem.

✻✻✻✻✻✻✻✻✻✻✻✻✻

Doctor, doctor, I keep thinking I'm a goat.
How long has this been happening?
Since I was a kid.

✻✻✻✻✻✻✻✻✻✻✻✻✻

Doctor, doctor, I think I'm a frog.
Hop it.

Doctor, doctor, I think I'm a squirrel.
You must be nuts.

Doctor, doctor, I think I've got woodworm.
How boring for you.

Doctor, doctor, I think I'm an elastic band.
Stretch yourself out on the couch then.

Doctor, doctor can you get rid of my spots, please?
I don't make rash promises.

Doctor, doctor, I've swallowed a roll of film.
Let's hope nothing serious develops.

Doctor, doctor, what can you give me for wind?
A kite?

Doctor, doctor, I'm a compulsive thief.

You better take something for that.

⁂

Doctor, doctor, can you help me out, please?

Certainly, the exit's that way.

⁂

Doctor, doctor, I keep seeing double.

Take a seat then. Which one?

⁂

Doctor, doctor people keep ignoring me.

Next.

⁂

Doctor, doctor, I've only got 59 seconds to live.

I'll see you in a minute.

⁂

Doctor, doctor, I feel like a bee.

Buzz off.

⁂

Doctor, doctor, I keep thinking I'm a desk.

You're just letting things get on top of you.

⁂

Doctor, doctor, I have a big strawberry on my head.

I'll give you some cream for that.

＊＊＊＊＊＊＊＊＊＊＊＊＊

Doctor, doctor, I smell like fish.

You poor sole.

＊＊＊＊＊＊＊＊＊＊＊＊＊

Doctor, doctor, I can't help frightening people.

Argggghhhhhh!

＊＊＊＊＊＊＊＊＊＊＊＊＊

Doctor, doctor I keep seeing a ladybird doing pirouettes.

Oh, that's just the bug that's going around.

＊＊＊＊＊＊＊＊＊＊＊＊＊

Doctor, doctor I'm suffering from a bad case of déjà vu.

I've seen you before.

＊＊＊＊＊＊＊＊＊＊＊＊＊

Doctor, doctor I feel like a violin.

Sit down while I make some notes.

＊＊＊＊＊＊＊＊＊＊＊＊＊

What time is it when you have to go to the dentist?

Tooth-hurtie

＊＊＊＊＊＊＊＊＊＊＊＊＊

Why did the boy creep past the medicine cabinet?

He didn't want to wake the sleeping pills.

How did the patient get to the doctor so quickly?

He flu.

What do you call someone who sits in a doctor's waiting room for hours and hours?

Patient.

What did the dentist say when the patient told him a terrible joke about his sweet tooth?

That's rotten.

What happens when dentists remove braces?

Their trousers fall down.

Why did the queen go to the dentist?

To get their tooth crowned.

Before my surgery, the anaesthesiologist offered to knock me out with gas or a boat paddle.

It was an ether/oar situation.

I didn't think orthopaedic shoes would help.

But I stand corrected.

⁎⁎⁎⁎⁎⁎⁎⁎⁎⁎⁎⁎⁎

Doctor, doctor, I have '70's fashion disease'.

It flares up now and again.

⁎⁎⁎⁎⁎⁎⁎⁎⁎⁎⁎⁎⁎

Doctor, doctor, I've got such a bad cold, and I have a feeling I had these exact same symptoms just recently.

It must be a case of deja flu.

⁎⁎⁎⁎⁎⁎⁎⁎⁎⁎⁎⁎⁎

If you have bladder problems.

Urine trouble.

⁎⁎⁎⁎⁎⁎⁎⁎⁎⁎⁎⁎⁎

Farts

What do you call a caveman's fart?

A blast from the past.

What do you get when a duke farts?

A noble gas.

Why wouldn't the skeleton fart in front of his friends?
He didn't have the guts.

Did you just fart?

Because you blew me away.

What do you call it when someone eats refried beans and onions?

Tear gas.

Why should you never fart in an elevator?

It's wrong on so many levels.

Why do horses like to fart when they race?

They can't achieve full horse power without gas.

Why did the comedian stop telling fart jokes?

Everyone told him they stink.

Food and Cooking

Why is a pancake like a cricket team?

They both need a good batter.

Why shouldn't you tell a secret on a farm?

Because the potatoes have eyes, the corn has ears, and the beans stalk.

What do you call a fake noodle?

An Impasta.

How do you make an apple turnover?

Push it downhill.

How do you make an apple puff?
Chase it around the kitchen.

⁎⁎⁎⁎⁎⁎⁎⁎⁎⁎⁎⁎

When's the best time of the day to eat a crisp apple?
Crunchtime.

⁎⁎⁎⁎⁎⁎⁎⁎⁎⁎⁎⁎

What did the butter say to the bread?
I'm on a roll!

⁎⁎⁎⁎⁎⁎⁎⁎⁎⁎⁎⁎

Why did the raisin go out with the prune?
She couldn't find a date.

⁎⁎⁎⁎⁎⁎⁎⁎⁎⁎⁎⁎

What does bread do after it's done baking?
Loaf around.

⁎⁎⁎⁎⁎⁎⁎⁎⁎⁎⁎⁎

How can you make a stew rich?
Add 14 carrots (carats) to it.

⁎⁎⁎⁎⁎⁎⁎⁎⁎⁎⁎⁎

Why did the Fungi leave the party?
There wasn't mushroom.

⁎⁎⁎⁎⁎⁎⁎⁎⁎⁎⁎⁎

Why did the Mushroom get invited to all the parties?
Because he's a fungi (fun guy).

Why do toadstools grow so closely together?
Because they don't have mushroom.

Did you hear about the angry pancake?
He just flipped.

What is the best day to eat ice-cream desserts?
Sundae.

What day do eggs hate most?
Fry-day

Where did the spaghetti go to dance?
The meat ball.

What's round, white and giggles?
A tickled onion.

Why did the chef serve frozen steak?
He wanted it to melt in the mouth.

How do you find prehistoric eggs?
With an eggscavator

What do you when you make a egg laugh?
You crack it up.

Why did the lemon stop rolling down the hill?
It ran out of juice.

Why were the little strawberries upset?
Because their parents were in a jam!

What did the plate say to the other plate?
Dinners on me tonight.

What did sushi A say to sushi B.
Waz up B? (wasabi).

What do you call a pig that does karate?

A pork chop.

⁎⁎⁎⁎⁎⁎⁎⁎⁎⁎⁎⁎

Why did the jelly wobble?

Because he saw the milk shake.

⁎⁎⁎⁎⁎⁎⁎⁎⁎⁎⁎⁎

How do you make a glass of milk shake?

Give it a fright.

⁎⁎⁎⁎⁎⁎⁎⁎⁎⁎⁎⁎

How do the Welsh eat cheese?

Caerphilly.

⁎⁎⁎⁎⁎⁎⁎⁎⁎⁎⁎⁎

How do you make a sausage roll?

Push it down a hill.

⁎⁎⁎⁎⁎⁎⁎⁎⁎⁎⁎⁎

What did the quick tomato say to the slow tomato?

Ketchup.

⁎⁎⁎⁎⁎⁎⁎⁎⁎⁎⁎⁎

What did the egg in the monastery say?

Out of the frying pan into the friar.

What happened to the rhubarb thief?

He ended up in custardy.

⁕⁕⁕⁕⁕⁕⁕⁕⁕⁕⁕⁕

What's the best thing to put in an apple pie?

A spoon.

⁕⁕⁕⁕⁕⁕⁕⁕⁕⁕⁕⁕

What's yellow and stupid?

Thick custard.

⁕⁕⁕⁕⁕⁕⁕⁕⁕⁕⁕⁕

How many decorations should you put on top of fairy cakes?

Hundreds and thousands.

⁕⁕⁕⁕⁕⁕⁕⁕⁕⁕⁕⁕

What stats with t, ends with t and is full of t?

A teapot.

⁕⁕⁕⁕⁕⁕⁕⁕⁕⁕⁕⁕

Why was the stale biscuit so sad?

He was feeling crummy.

⁕⁕⁕⁕⁕⁕⁕⁕⁕⁕⁕⁕

Why did the biscuit cry?

His mum was a wafer so long.

⁕⁕⁕⁕⁕⁕⁕⁕⁕⁕⁕⁕

Why did the man eat yeast and furniture polish for breakfast?

He wanted to rise and shine.

⁂

Why did the tomato go red?

He saw the salad dressing.

⁂

Why couldn't the poppy seed leave the bowling alley?

He was on a roll.

⁂

Why did the man eat at the investment bank?

He loved rich food.

⁂

What did the sherbert say to the humbug?

"Hi, sweetie!"

⁂

Why did the cream squeal?

Someone was whipping it.

⁂

Why did the bacon laugh?

Because the egg cracked a yolk.

What beef only comes in 2, 3, 5, 7, or 11 ounce portions?

Prime rib.

I'm allergic to bread but eat it anyway.

I'm a gluten for punishment.

What do you call a helpful lemon?

Lemonaid.

I recently switched all the labels on my wife's spice rack.

She hasn't realised yet, but the thyme is cumin.

People are so sad I'm not entering the bake off this year.

Even their cakes are in tiers.

I said to the baker, "How come all your cakes are 50p, but that one's £1?"

He said, "That's Madeira cake".

I really don't want to see puns about French eggs anymore.

Un oeuf is un oeuf.

⁎⁎⁎⁎⁎⁎⁎⁎⁎⁎⁎⁎⁎

I've just created an everlasting lemon.

It's given me a real zest for life.

⁎⁎⁎⁎⁎⁎⁎⁎⁎⁎⁎⁎⁎

Personally, I think tofu is overrated.

It's just a curd to me.

⁎⁎⁎⁎⁎⁎⁎⁎⁎⁎⁎⁎⁎

I went to the zoo yesterday and I saw a piece of toast in a cage.

When I asked the keeper why?

Apparently, It was bread in captivity.

⁎⁎⁎⁎⁎⁎⁎⁎⁎⁎⁎⁎⁎

I didn't understand what my wife meant when she told me I was holding the bag of pasta upside down.

And then the penne dropped.

⁎⁎⁎⁎⁎⁎⁎⁎⁎⁎⁎⁎⁎

The man who created the chickpea spread passed away but has been given an award posthummusly.

I bought my depressed friend a Chinese takeaway to cheer him up.

I passed him the soy sauce and it upset him even more.

You should never Kikkoman when he's down.

⁎⁎⁎⁎⁎⁎⁎⁎⁎⁎⁎⁎⁎

What did the cheese say to itself in the mirror?

Halloumi.

⁎⁎⁎⁎⁎⁎⁎⁎⁎⁎⁎⁎⁎

The recipe said, "Set the oven to 180 degrees."

Now I have no idea what to do, because the oven door is facing the wall.

⁎⁎⁎⁎⁎⁎⁎⁎⁎⁎⁎⁎⁎

I read a study the other day claiming that "humans eat more bananas than monkeys".

Which - to me - sounded a bit obvious. I can't remember the last time I ate a monkey.

⁎⁎⁎⁎⁎⁎⁎⁎⁎⁎⁎⁎⁎

Walking home last night, I passed a slice of apple pie, an ice cream sundae, and a lemon cheesecake.

I thought to myself, "The streets seem strangely desserted."

⁎⁎⁎⁎⁎⁎⁎⁎⁎⁎⁎⁎⁎

What do you call a chicken looking at a bowl of lettuce.

Chicken sees a salad.

⁎⁎⁎⁎⁎⁎⁎⁎⁎⁎⁎⁎⁎

How do you fix a cracked pumpkin?

With a pumpkin patch.

⁎⁕⁕⁕⁕⁕⁕⁕⁕⁕⁕⁕⁎

What noise does a nut make when it sneezes?

Cashew.

⁎⁕⁕⁕⁕⁕⁕⁕⁕⁕⁕⁕⁎

What fruit never gets lonely?

A pear.

⁎⁕⁕⁕⁕⁕⁕⁕⁕⁕⁕⁕⁎

Did you hear about the Italian chef who died recently?

He just pasta way so quickly. But hey, you cannoli do so much. His life will remain a pizza history.

⁎⁕⁕⁕⁕⁕⁕⁕⁕⁕⁕⁕⁎

The pizza chef burnt the Hawaiian pizza.

He should have use Aloha temperature.

⁎⁕⁕⁕⁕⁕⁕⁕⁕⁕⁕⁕⁎

Sneezed all over my toast.

Can't believe it snot butter...

⁎⁕⁕⁕⁕⁕⁕⁕⁕⁕⁕⁕⁎

My wife insisted on pouring flour into the melted butter.

I told her she would roux the day.

⁎⁕⁕⁕⁕⁕⁕⁕⁕⁕⁕⁕⁎

Friends and Family

Ever wondered what to say to your sister when she's crying?

"Are you having a crisis?"

I warned my daughter about using her whistle inside the house today and gave her one last chance.

Unfortunately, she blew it.

My next door neighbour and I are good friends, so we decided to share our water supply.

We got a long well.

My dad was born as a conjoined twin, but the doctors managed to separate them at birth.

I have an uncle, once removed.

⁕⁕⁕⁕⁕⁕⁕⁕⁕⁕⁕⁕⁕

Going into my teenage son's bedroom is like a trip to IKEA...

I went in for a look and came out with 6 cups, 4 plates, 3 bowls and some cutlery...

⁕⁕⁕⁕⁕⁕⁕⁕⁕⁕⁕⁕⁕

Bought my friend an elephant for his room.

He said 'Thanks.'

I said don't mention it.

⁕⁕⁕⁕⁕⁕⁕⁕⁕⁕⁕⁕⁕

My Nan used to say "Take everything with a pinch of salt".

Lovely lady, made terrible tea though.

⁕⁕⁕⁕⁕⁕⁕⁕⁕⁕⁕⁕⁕

My mate confessed to me that he has a weird habit of colouring in the tops of people's arms.

I think he was just looking for a shoulder to crayon...

⁕⁕⁕⁕⁕⁕⁕⁕⁕⁕⁕⁕⁕

My friend works in IT and I asked him, "How do you make a motherboard?"

He said, "I usually tell her about my job."

⁕⁕⁕⁕⁕⁕⁕⁕⁕⁕⁕⁕⁕

I asked my dad, "Can we get some pets?"

He said: "No, pets are just a step backwards."

⁎⁎⁎⁎⁎⁎⁎⁎⁎⁎⁎⁎

My neighbour rang on my doorbell at 3am. Can you believe it!?

Luckily I was still up playing the drums.

⁎⁎⁎⁎⁎⁎⁎⁎⁎⁎⁎⁎

I asked Dad how he plans to spend the day. He said, "First, Mum and I will go pick up our prescription glasses"

"And then we'll see."

⁎⁎⁎⁎⁎⁎⁎⁎⁎⁎⁎⁎

I've been saying "mucho" to my Spanish friend a lot more often lately.

It means a lot to him.

⁎⁎⁎⁎⁎⁎⁎⁎⁎⁎⁎⁎

My neighbour and I became good friends, so we decided to rent a space together to park our cars.

We have a lot in common.

⁎⁎⁎⁎⁎⁎⁎⁎⁎⁎⁎⁎

Dad, are we pyromaniacs?

Yes, we arson.

⁎⁎⁎⁎⁎⁎⁎⁎⁎⁎⁎⁎

Why did the wife divorce the baker?

Because he was too kneady.

I told my daughter, "Go to bed, the cows are sleeping in the field."

She said, "What's that got to do with anything?"

I said "That means it's pasture bedtime."

My son accidentally smashed his foot on the table. As he was hopping around the room, I picked up my phone and asked him, "Do you want me to call..."

"...a toe truck?"

Geography

Did you hear about the cheese factory explosion in France?

All that was left was de Brie.

⁕⁕⁕⁕⁕⁕⁕⁕⁕⁕⁕⁕

There's a lot of cities in France, like Paris, Marseilles, or Lyon.

But there's only one city that's Nice.

⁕⁕⁕⁕⁕⁕⁕⁕⁕⁕⁕⁕

I tripped in France.

Eiffel over.

⁕⁕⁕⁕⁕⁕⁕⁕⁕⁕⁕⁕

British people be like: I'm bri'ish.

I guess they drank the t.

⁕⁕⁕⁕⁕⁕⁕⁕⁕⁕⁕⁕

My friend Ty came first in the Beijing marathon, but he wasn't given the gold medal.

The Chinese authorities refused to recognise Ty Won.

※※※※※※※※※※※

"I went to a terrible gig in South East Asia the other day."

"Singapore?"

"Yeah she had a shocking voice".

※※※※※※※※※※※

I used to have an invisible friend from Korea.

My mum said it was just my imagine Asian.

※※※※※※※※※※※

I've found a chip shop in West London that serves its fish on photocopier paper.

It's a little plaice on the A4.

※※※※※※※※※※※

The Spanish King has been quarantined on his private jet.

This means that the reign in Spain will stay mainly on the plane.

※※※※※※※※※※※

My Himalayan friend has a bull that refuses to stand up.

I always see Himalayan there.

※※※※※※※※※※※

Why is Europe like a dirty frying pan?
It has Greece at the bottom.

What do you call the small rivers that run into the Nile?
Juveniles.

Which capital city cheats in exams?
Peking.

Where would you find Oslo?
On a map.

In which city can you wander around aimlessly?
Rome.

What's the coldest place in the world?
Chile.

What's the best thing to take to the desert?
A thirst-aid kit.

A Samoan man gave me a detailed history and explanation of his heritage, culture, and the country in which he was raised

Those specific islanders!

⁎⁕⁕⁕⁕⁕⁕⁕⁕⁕⁎

My wife's just gone to the West Indies.

Jamaica?

No, she went of her own accord.

⁎⁕⁕⁕⁕⁕⁕⁕⁕⁕⁎

We've just been for a holiday in the South of England.

In Dorset?

Oh yes, we thoroughly recommend it.

⁎⁕⁕⁕⁕⁕⁕⁕⁕⁕⁎

Where's your daughter going on holiday this year?

Alaska.

No, don't bother her, I just thought you'd know.

⁎⁕⁕⁕⁕⁕⁕⁕⁕⁕⁎

Ghost Jokes

I think the ghost in the chicken coop was a poultrygheist.

Why are Ghosts rubbish at lying?

You can see right through them.

What did the Hungarian ghost eat for dinner?

Ghoulash.

What's a ghost's favourite dessert?

I scream.

What kind of key does a ghost use to unlock his room?
A spoo-key.

What do ghosts eat for supper?
Spooketi.

What is a ghost's favourite dessert?
Booberry pie.

Why are graveyards noisy?
Because of all the coffin!

What do you call a dancing ghost?
Polka-haunt-us

Where does a ghost go on Saturday night?
Anywhere where he can boo-gie.

Two ghosts walk into a bar, the bartender said.
"Sorry but we don't serve spirits."

What do ghosts use on their hair?
Shamboo!

What do you call a ghost with a broken leg?
A Hoblin Goblin.

What did the ghost teacher say to the class?
Look at the board and I'll go through it again.

What do you call a ghost comedian?
Dead funny.

What tool helps ghosts lie perfectly flat?
A spirit level.

What are a ghost's favourite rides at the fair?
The scary-go-round and rollerghoster.

History Jokes

What was Camelot famous for?

Its knight life.

Who invented Sir Arthur's round table?

Sir Cumference.

Have you ever seen a picture of Mount Rushmore before it was carved?

It was unpresidented.

Why did the drowning Pharaoh refuse to ask for help?

He was in de Nile.

Why was the Pharaoh boastful?

Because he sphinx he's the best.

How did brave Ancient Egyptians write?

With hero-glyphics.

How do you use an ancient Egyptian doorbell?

Toot and come in.

What was the most popular kids' movie in Ancient Greece?

Troy Story.

A Roman walks into a bar. He holds up two fingers and says, "Five beers, please!"

Which famous Roman suffered from hayfever?

Julius Sneezer.

How was the Roman Empire cut in half?

With a pair of Caesars.

How did Vikings send secret messages?

By Norse code.

・●●●●●●●●●●●・

Why is the Medieval period often called the Dark Ages?

Because there were so many knights.

・●●●●●●●●●●●・

Why did Henry VIII struggle to breathe?

He had no heir.

・●●●●●●●●●●●・

Why was Elizabethan England so wet?

Because the Queen reigned for 45 years.

・●●●●●●●●●●●・

If April showers bring May flowers, what do May flowers bring?

The Pilgrims.

・●●●●●●●●●●●・

Two wrongs don't make a right, but what do two Wrights make?

An aeroplane.

・●●●●●●●●●●●・

I've recently started to learn about the history of chess boards

Seems they have quite the checkered past.

∙∙∙∙∙∙∙∙∙∙∙∙∙

What yearbook superlative was Robert E. Lee given at graduation?

Most likely to secede.

∙∙∙∙∙∙∙∙∙∙∙∙∙

How did Louis XIV feel after completing the Palace of Versailles?

Baroque.

∙∙∙∙∙∙∙∙∙∙∙∙∙

Who invented fire?

Some bright spark.

∙∙∙∙∙∙∙∙∙∙∙∙∙

What happened when the wheel was invented?

It caused a revolution.

∙∙∙∙∙∙∙∙∙∙∙∙∙

Jokes

Two drunk guys were fighting. One of them drew a line in the dirt, and said if the other crossed it they would punch them in the face.

That was the punchline.

Did you hear the joke about the broken egg?

Yes, it cracked me up.

Fart jokes are funny but eye jokes are cornea.

Have you heard the joke about the butter?

I better not tell you, it might spread.

Did you hear the joke about the peach?

It was pit-iful.

Have you heard the joke about the spade?

It's ground-breaking.

Have you heard the joke about the bed?

Sorry, it hasn't been made yet.

Have you heard the joke about the butter?

I'm sorry, I can't tell you, you might spread it.

Jokes about German sausages...

Are the wurst.

It's inappropriate to make a 'dad joke' if you're not a dad.

It's a faux pa.

Have you heard the latest statistics joke?

Probably.

Did you hear the joke about the piece of paper?

Don't worry about it, it's tearable.

When does a joke become a "dad" joke?

When the punchline is a parent.

I was going to see if I had a clean but funny joke about oil but they are all a bit crude.

Have you heard the joke about the blunt pencil?

I'd tell you, but there's no point.

I like jokes about the eyes.

The cornea the better.

I'd tell you a joke about space, but…

It's too, out of this world!

Puns about exit signs?

They are on the way out.

Have you heard the joke about the dustbin?
It's rubbish.

⁎⁎⁎⁎⁎⁎⁎⁎⁎⁎⁎

Have you heard the joke about the drill?
It's boring.

⁎⁎⁎⁎⁎⁎⁎⁎⁎⁎⁎

Have you heard the joke about the cheese biscuit?
It's a cracker.

⁎⁎⁎⁎⁎⁎⁎⁎⁎⁎⁎

Have you heard the joke about the skunk?
It stinks.

⁎⁎⁎⁎⁎⁎⁎⁎⁎⁎⁎

Have you heard the joke about the fence?
I just can't get over it.

⁎⁎⁎⁎⁎⁎⁎⁎⁎⁎⁎

Have you heard the joke about the vacuum cleaner?
It sucks.

⁎⁎⁎⁎⁎⁎⁎⁎⁎⁎⁎

Have you heard the joke about the horse with a sore foot?
It's a bit lame.

⁎⁎⁎⁎⁎⁎⁎⁎⁎⁎⁎

Lightbulb Jokes

How many sopranos does it take to change a lightbulb?

One – she just holds on and the world revolves around her.

How many musicians does it take to change a light bulb?

Twenty. 1 to hold the bulb, 2 to turn the ladder, and 17 to be on the guest list.

How many folk musicians does it take to change a light bulb?

Seven; one to change and the other six to sing about how good the old one was.

How many blues musicians does it take to change a lightbulb?

Five. One to screw in the lightbulb, and four to play sad, blue songs about the old, worn-out lightbulb.

⁂

How many elves does it take to change a lightbulb?

Ten. One to change the bulb and nine underneath him, standing on each other's shoulders.

⁂

How many birds does it take to change a light bulb?

Toucan do it.

⁂

How many Psychiatrists does it take to change a light bulb?

Only one, but the bulb has got to really want to change.

⁂

How many programmers does it take to screw in a light bulb?

None. That's a hardware problem.

⁂

How many graduate students does it take to change a light bulb?

Only one, but it takes nine years.

How many professors does it take to change a light bulb?

Only one, but they get three technical reports out of it.

⁂

How many bureaucrats does it take to screw in a light bulb?

Two. One to assure the everything possible is being done while the other screws the bulb into the water faucet.

⁂

How many board meetings does it take to get a light bulb changed?

This topic was resumed from last week's discussion, but is incomplete pending resolution of some action items. It will be continued next week. Meanwhile...

⁂

How many politicians does it take to change a light bulb?

What sort of answer did you have in mind?

⁂

How many lawyers does it take to change a light bulb?

How many can you afford?

⁂

How many actors does it take to change a light bulb?

Only one. They don't like to share the spotlight.

⁂

How many admin assistants does it take to change a lightbulb ?

None. I can't do anything unless you complete a lightbulb design change request form.

How many art directors does it take to change a lightbulb?

Does it have to be a lightbulb?

How many movie actresses does it take to change a lightbulb?

Eleven. One to hold the lightbulb and the rest to turn the room around her.

How many journalists does it take to screw in a light bulb?

Only one, but he'll tell everybody.

How many nuclear engineers does it take to change a light bulb?

Seven. One to install the new bulb and six to figure out what to do with the old one for the next 10,000 years.

How many optimists does it take to screw in a light bulb?

None, they're convinced that the light will come back on soon.

⁎⁎⁎⁎⁎⁎⁎⁎⁎⁎⁎⁎

How many pessimists does it take to screw in a light bulb?

None, it's a waste of time because the new bulb probably won't work either.

⁎⁎⁎⁎⁎⁎⁎⁎⁎⁎⁎⁎

How many philosophers does it take to change a lightbulb ?

Define "change."

⁎⁎⁎⁎⁎⁎⁎⁎⁎⁎⁎⁎

How many quantum mechanics does it take to change a light bulb?

They can't. If they know where the socket is, they cannot locate the new bulb.

⁎⁎⁎⁎⁎⁎⁎⁎⁎⁎⁎⁎

How many statisticians does it take to change a lightbulb ?

Four -- plus or minus three

⁎⁎⁎⁎⁎⁎⁎⁎⁎⁎⁎⁎

How many surgeons does it take to change a light bulb?

None. They would wait for a suitable donor and do a filament transplant.

⁂

How many surrealists does it take to change a light bulb?

Two. One to hold the giraffe and the other to fill the bathtub with brightly coloured machine tools.

⁂

How many teenagers does it take to screw in a light bulb?

One, but they'll be on the phone for five hours telling all their friends about it.

⁂

How many cover blurb writers does it take to screw in a lightbulb?

A vast and teeming horde stretching from sea to shining sea!

⁂

How many chickens does it take to change a lightbulb?

None, they're too busy crossing the road.

⁂

How many crime writers does it take to change a lightbulb?

Two. One to screw it in and the other to give it a good twist at the end.

⁎⊛⊛⊛⊛⊛⊛⊛⊛⊛⊛⁎

How many police officers does it take to change a lightbulb?

None. It turned itself in.

⁎⊛⊛⊛⊛⊛⊛⊛⊛⊛⊛⁎

How many shop assistants does it take to change a lightbulb?

One as long as you have the receipt.

⁎⊛⊛⊛⊛⊛⊛⊛⊛⊛⊛⁎

Magic Jokes

What do you get when you cross an airplane with a magician?

A flying sorcerer.

What happened when the magician got mad?

She pulled her hare out!

Did you hear about the magical tractor?

It turned into a field.

Did you hear about the magician who uses chocolate in his magic act?

He's always got a couple of twix up his sleeve...

What does a condiment wizard perform?

Saucery.

Marriage and Relationship Jokes

My wife says I only have 2 faults.

I don't listen - and something else.

My wife said she'd leave me if I didn't stop eating pasta.

Now I'm feeling cannelloni.

My wife left a note on the fridge saying: "This isn't working. I'm leaving."

"What a lie! I opened the fridge door and it's working fine."

I told my wife she should embrace her mistakes.

She gave me a hug.

My wife told me to stop acting like a flamingo.

So I had to put my foot down.

⁕⁕⁕⁕⁕⁕⁕⁕⁕⁕⁕

My wife is like a newspaper.

There is a new issue every day.

⁕⁕⁕⁕⁕⁕⁕⁕⁕⁕⁕

My wife said she's leaving me because of my obsession with tennis - and I'm too old.

I said: "I'm only 40 love."

⁕⁕⁕⁕⁕⁕⁕⁕⁕⁕⁕

My wife complains I don't buy her flowers.

To be honest, I didn't know she sold flowers.

⁕⁕⁕⁕⁕⁕⁕⁕⁕⁕⁕

My girlfriend gets mad whenever I mess with her red wine.

So I added fruit and lemonade to it and now she's sangria then ever.

⁕⁕⁕⁕⁕⁕⁕⁕⁕⁕⁕

I was on the phone with my wife and said, "I'm almost home, honey, please put the coffee maker on."
After a twenty second pause, I asked, "You still there sweetheart?"

"Yes..." she said. "But I don't think the coffee maker wants to talk right now."

⁕⁕⁕⁕⁕⁕⁕⁕⁕⁕⁕

How do you get a country girl's attention?

A tractor.

●●●●●●●●●●●●●

My wife said she's leaving me because of my continual puns about flowers.

I said "where's does this stem from petal?"

●●●●●●●●●●●●●

At my wedding I was let down by the caterers and all we had to eat were sugar coated cornflakes.

It was a bit of a Frostie reception.

●●●●●●●●●●●●●

So I said to my wife "Would you like a Kit-Kat Chunky?"

Over five hours in A&E...

●●●●●●●●●●●●●

My wife is kicking me out because she's fed up with my South American animal puns...

'OK,' I said, 'Alpaca my bags.'

●●●●●●●●●●●●●

I once got dumped by a girlfriend because she discovered I had belonged to a chess club.

She found out about my chequered past.

●●●●●●●●●●●●●

The wife just threw six cricket balls at me.

"What's up ?" I asked.

"It's over," she replied.

⁕⁕⁕⁕⁕⁕⁕⁕⁕⁕⁕⁕⁕

My wife keeps empty margarine tubs and just leaves them lying around.

I can't believe it's not clutter.

⁕⁕⁕⁕⁕⁕⁕⁕⁕⁕⁕⁕⁕

Last night I gave my wife my medieval battle uniform to polish while I went to the pub.

She's always said she wanted a night in, shining armour.

⁕⁕⁕⁕⁕⁕⁕⁕⁕⁕⁕⁕⁕

My wife bought a new oven glove in a bright yellow colour.

I kept making puns about it, and now she's not talking to me.

I probably did take it too far, I mustard mitt.

⁕⁕⁕⁕⁕⁕⁕⁕⁕⁕⁕⁕⁕

My wife tripped and fell while carrying clothes she just ironed.

I watched it all unfold.

⁕⁕⁕⁕⁕⁕⁕⁕⁕⁕⁕⁕⁕

My wife emailed me our wedding photos, but I couldn't open any of the files.

I always have trouble with emotional attachments.

⁜⁜⁜⁜⁜⁜⁜⁜⁜⁜⁜

My wife was a little puzzled when I suddenly bought some new beads for her abacus. Smiling, I said to her.

"Honey, it's the little things that count!"

⁜⁜⁜⁜⁜⁜⁜⁜⁜⁜⁜

My wife told me, "Don't get upset if people call you fat."

You're much bigger than that.

⁜⁜⁜⁜⁜⁜⁜⁜⁜⁜⁜

If I send a clown to deliver flowers to my wife.

Is that a romantic jester?

⁜⁜⁜⁜⁜⁜⁜⁜⁜⁜⁜

My girlfriend and I have been together for 10 years, but I never heard her tell a single joke.

We are in a very serious relationship.

⁜⁜⁜⁜⁜⁜⁜⁜⁜⁜⁜

I hate when my wife gets mad at me for being lazy.

It's not like I did anything.

⁜⁜⁜⁜⁜⁜⁜⁜⁜⁜⁜

Yesterday my wife thought she saw a cockroach in the kitchen, she sprayed everything down and cleaned thoroughly.

Today I'm putting a cockroach in the bathroom.

⁂

I hate it when my wife says "Are you listening to me?!"

Such a random way to start a conversation.

⁂

My wife sent me a text that read, "If you're sleeping, send me your dreams. If you're laughing, send me your smile. If you're eating, send me a bite. If you're drinking, send me a sip. If you're crying, send me your tears. I love you!"

I replied: "I'm on the toilet please advise."

⁂

My wife said that quilts are better than duvets.

I told her to be careful making blanket statements like that.

⁂

I met my boyfriend while visiting the zoo. There he was, in his uniform.

Right away I knew he was a keeper.

⁂

Why should you never date a tennis player?

Because love means nothing to them.

⁂

Maths Jokes

What do you call a number that won't keep still?

A Roamin' numeral.

Why can't your nose be 12 inches long?

Because then it would be a foot!

Have you heard the one about the student who was afraid of negative numbers?

He'll stop at nothing to avoid them.

If you have 7 apples in one hand and 5 apples in the other, what do you have?

Big hands

How do you make seven an even number?

Take the s out!

• • • • • • • • • • • • •

Why should the number 288 never be mentioned?

It's two gross.

• • • • • • • • • • • • •

Why is 6 afraid of 7?

Because 7 ate 9!

• • • • • • • • • • • • •

How do you count cows?

With a cowculator.

• • • • • • • • • • • • •

What did math book say to the other?

Don't bother me I've got my own problems!

• • • • • • • • • • • • •

What do mathematicians eat on Halloween?

Pumpkin Pi.

• • • • • • • • • • • • •

Why did the girl wear glasses during math class?

Because it improves di-vison.

• • • • • • • • • • • • •

What geometric figure is like a lost parrot?

A polygon.

Why did the boy eat his math homework?

Because the teacher told him it was a piece of cake.

What snakes are good at doing sums?

Adders

How can you make time fly?

Throw a clock out the window.

Why did the two 4's skip lunch?

They already 8.

What did the triangle say to the circle?

You're pointless.

Why can't a nose be 12 inches long?

Because then it would be a foot.

Why do mathematicians like parks?

Because of all the natural logs.

How do mathematicians tell off their children?

"If I've told you n times, I've told you n+1 times..."

What did the set square say to the protractor?

Take me to your ruler.

Why don't cannibals like the sum four plus four?

Because they get eight.

Which animals are best at maths?

Rabbits, they can multiply really quickly.

What tools come in handy during a maths lesson?

Multi-pliers.

What's a mathematician's favourite meal?

Pi.

I had a hen who could count her own eggs.

She's a mathmachicken.

Why is 16 always full?

Because it 8 and 8.

I, for one, am a big fan of Roman numeral puns.

A pie factory has exploded injuring 4 members of staff.

The blast was heard 3.14159 miles away.

What do you get if you divide 22 sheep into 7 pens?

A shepherd's pi.

Last night I dreamt I was trying to divide 10 by 3.

It's a recurring dream.

What did 2 tell 3 when he saw 6 acting like an idiot?

Don't mind him. He is just a product of our times.

Why didn't 4 ask out 5.

Because he was 2^2.

⋆⋆⋆⋆⋆⋆⋆⋆⋆⋆⋆⋆⋆

Did you know that 97% of the world is stupid?

Luckily I'm in the other 5%.

⋆⋆⋆⋆⋆⋆⋆⋆⋆⋆⋆⋆⋆

Don't have an argument with Pi.

He's irrational.

⋆⋆⋆⋆⋆⋆⋆⋆⋆⋆⋆⋆⋆

Miscellaneous Jokes

What do you call a door that is cute?

Adorable.

What's white, furry and smells of peppermint?

A polo bear.

Why didn't the teddy bear eat his lunch?

He was already stuffed.

Why don't you wear a cardboard belt?

That would be a waist of paper.

What did the hat say to the scarf?

You hang around and I'll go on ahead.

What's did one tomato say to the other tomato?

You go ahead and I'll ketchup.

Why did the man start liking facial hair?

It just grew on him.

What happened to the man who was addicted to soap?

He's clean now.

What happened to the man who tried to catch the fog?

He mist.

Why are management meetings so terribly dull?

They're held in the bored room.

What did one lift say to the other lift?

I think I'm coming down with something.

If you found money in every pocket of a pair of trousers, what would you have?

Someone else's trousers.

⁂

Why wouldn't the bald man lend anyone his comb?

He couldn't part with it.

⁂

Why couldn't the frightened archer hit the target?

His arrows were all in a quiver.

⁂

What did one eye say to the other eye?

Before you and me, something smells.

⁂

I've been diagnosed with a chronic fear of giants.

Feefiphobia.

⁂

I want to tell you about a girl who only eats plants.

You've probably never heard of herbivore.

⁂

Did you hear about the ATM that got addicted to money?

It suffered from withdrawals.

⁂

I debated a flat earther once. He stormed off saying he'd walk to the edge of the Earth to prove me wrong.

He'll come round - eventually.

⁂

To ride a horse or not to ride a horse.

That is equestrian.

⁂

I dreamed I saw a colour I never saw before.

It was just a pigment of my imagination.

⁂

My nickname at work is Mr. Compromise.

It wasn't my first choice but I'm ok with it.

⁂

A lumberjack went in to a magic forest to cut a tree. Upon arrival, he started to swing at the tree, when it shouted, "Wait! I'm a talking tree!"

The lumberjack grinned: "And you will dialogue."

⁂

Is it crazy how saying sentences backwards...

creates...

backwards sentences saying how crazy it is?

How do you make a waterbed more bouncy?

Add spring water.

***

What does a house wear?

Address.

***

My nerdy friend just got a PhD on the history of palindromes.

He's really good, knows his stuff forwards and backwards.

***

I bought a knife that can cut through four loaves of bread at once.

It's a four loaf cleaver.

***

I'm thinking of colouring my hair, keeping it short at the front and sides but growing it long at the back.

It sounds a bit like a do or dye situation but I'm going to take time to mullet over.

***

I once had an interesting conversation with a very profound overweight monk.

He was a deep fat friar.

Apparently there's a new superhero called 'Aluminium Man.'

He goes around foiling crime.

• •••••••••• •

I used to work in a factory making snow globes and I fell into one of the machines.

Luckily I wasn't badly hurt, just quite shaken up.

• •••••••••• •

I once accidentally locked myself inside a glass cabinet in a museum.

Ended up making a complete exhibition of myself.

• •••••••••• •

I've had such a bad day.

First I got into fight with a guy dressed as Shakespeare, then I almost choked on a German sausage.

It's gone from bard to wurst...

• •••••••••• •

My friend got badly hurt making butter on his farm.

It was a really unfortunate churn of events.

• •••••••••• •

80% of my couch fell on my foot today.

Ouch.

• •••••••••• •

If Watson isn't the most famous doctor.

Then Who is.

●●●●●●●●●●●●

To keep fit, I've taken up quiet tennis.

It's like regular tennis, but without the racquet.

●●●●●●●●●●●●

Will glass coffins ever become popular?

Remains to be seen.

●●●●●●●●●●●●

What should you do if you are addicted to sea weed?

Sea kelp

●●●●●●●●●●●●

What do you call an apology written in dots and dashes?

Re-morse code.

●●●●●●●●●●●●

I tried to use the army toilets, but one of the officers stopped me and said, "It'll cost you $10 to go in there."

I'm the loo tenant.

●●●●●●●●●●●●

Are people born with a photographic memory?

Or does it take time to develop?

●●●●●●●●●●●●

Money

What do you call a belt made out of hundred dollar bills?

A waist of money.

I'm never again donating money to anyone collecting for a marathon.

They just take the money and run.

My wife says I'm tight, so to prove her wrong I'm taking her out for tea and biscuits today.

It should be quite exciting as she's never given blood before.

How many dollars does it cost pirates to get their ears pierced?

About a buccaneer.

Monsters, dragons and other fictitious creatures

Why do dragons sleep during the day?

They work the knight shift.

What does the Loch Ness Monster say to the salmon?

"Long time, no sea."

Did you hear about the very clever monster?

He was called Frank Einstein.

What do you do with a blue monster?

Try and cheer it up.

Why couldn't the ghost order a vodka at the bar?
They didn't serve spirits.

Where do you find giant snails?
At the end of the giant's fingers.

What happened when the ghosts went on strike?
A skeleton crew took over.

What's the best way to speak to a scary monster?
Long-distance.

How does a monster count to 17?
On his fingers.

Why did the monster's mother knit him three socks?
She heard he grew another foot.

What is Dracula's favourite circus act?
The juggler.

What do you do if you want to learn more about Dracula?

You join his fang club.

※※※※※※※※※※※

What is a vampire's favourite dance?

The Fang-Dango.

※※※※※※※※※※※

Why are vampires so easy to fool?

Because they're suckers.

※※※※※※※※※※※

Why did the dragon breathe on a map of the earth?

Because he wanted to set the world on fire.

※※※※※※※※※※※

Imagine if vampires had blunt teeth and couldn't bite you?

They would just suck.

※※※※※※※※※※※

Mummy Jokes

Why don't mummies take vacations?

They're afraid they'll relax and unwind.

Whatmusic do mummies listen to?

Wrap music.

Where do mummies go for a swim?

To the dead sea.

Why do mummies have so much trouble keeping friends?

They're too wrapped up in themselves.

Why was the mummy so tense?

He was all wound up.

⁂

What is mummy's favourite kind of coffee?

De-coffin-ated.

⁂

How do you use an ancient Egyptian doorbell?

Toot-and-come-in.

⁂

What's a mummy's favourite music?

Ragtime.

⁂

Archaeologists in Egypt have unearthed a tomb containing a mummy covered in chocolate & nuts.

Excited they believe it is the remains of the long lost Pharaoh Roche.

⁂

What do you get if you cross an Egyptian mummy with a car mechanic?

Toot and Car Man.

Music Jokes

Why couldn't the string quartet find their composer?

He was Haydn.

There are so many jokes about this composer.

I could make you a Liszt.

How do you fix a broken brass instrument?

With a tuba glue.

What do you get when you drop a piano down a mine shaft?

A flat miner.

A, C and E walk into a bar.

"Sorry," the barman says, "we don't serve minors."

⁕ ⁕⁕⁕⁕⁕⁕⁕⁕⁕⁕⁕

Did you see the sign outside the music shop?

"Gone Chopin. Be Bach in a minuet."

⁕ ⁕⁕⁕⁕⁕⁕⁕⁕⁕⁕⁕

How do you make a bandstand?

You take away the chairs.

⁕ ⁕⁕⁕⁕⁕⁕⁕⁕⁕⁕⁕

What type of music are balloons scared of?

Pop music.

⁕ ⁕⁕⁕⁕⁕⁕⁕⁕⁕⁕⁕

Why did the singer climb the ladder?

To reach the high notes.

⁕ ⁕⁕⁕⁕⁕⁕⁕⁕⁕⁕⁕

What was stolen from the music store?

The lute.

⁕ ⁕⁕⁕⁕⁕⁕⁕⁕⁕⁕⁕

What musical instrument would a cucumber play?

A pickle-o.

⁕ ⁕⁕⁕⁕⁕⁕⁕⁕⁕⁕⁕

What did Beethoven do when he died?

He decomposed!

What kind of music do planets sing?

Neptunes.

What do you call a musician with problems?

A trebled man.

What do you get if you put a radio in the fridge?

Cool music.

Why did the codebreaker spend so long in the percussion section?

He was looking for cymbals.

I used to be in a band called "The Hinges"

We opened for "The Doors."

Whilst holidaying in France, there was a group of mushrooms singing Queen covers.

I said, "You're really brilliant. What's your band called?"

Lead singer replied, "Weeee are the champignons my friend."

Puns about 'Riverdance'?

I Flatley refuse to say them.

For my next trick, I will eat a percussion instrument in a bap.

Drum roll please.

The urge for me to sing "The Lion Sleeps Tonight."

. . .is only ever a whim away.

My friend has invited me to go to the opera tomorrow to watch 'Carmen'.

I'd like to go but I'm already Bizet.

I'm opening a new 'David Bowie themed' curry house.

'Spice Oddity.'

I write songs about sewing machines.

I'm a singer songwriter.

●●●●●●●●●●●●

Well I paid £10 for a Dire Straits album and the download was completely blank.

Money for nothing.

●●●●●●●●●●●●

Apparently, there's a place in the Czech Republic where they do hip-hop covers of Queen songs.

It's the Bohemian Rap City.

●●●●●●●●●●●●

My friend called me for help, claiming he had turned into a harp.

I raced over there only to find he was a lyre.

●●●●●●●●●●●●

What type of music do rabbits like best?

Hip hop.

●●●●●●●●●●●●

What's the definition of Baroque?

When you run out of Monet.

●●●●●●●●●●●●

Planes, Trains and Automobiles

A truck loaded with Vicks Vaporub overturned on the highway.

Amazingly, there was no congestion for eight hours.

※※※※※※※※※※※

What's the difference between a poorly dressed man on a tricycle and a well dressed man on a bicycle?

Attire.

※※※※※※※※※※※

New idea: invisible aircraft.

I can't see that taking off.

※※※※※※※※※※※

An ice cream van crashed down our road.

The whole area is coned off.

※※※※※※※※※※※

BREAKING: A lorry load of sugar and a van containing strawberries have crashed on the M1 this morning.

A traffic spokesperson has reported that motorists will suffer major delays due the enormous jam it's created.

●●●●●●●●●●●●

I have a new job transporting shallots on slow moving boats along canals.

I'm an onion bargee.

●●●●●●●●●●●●

BREAKING: a lorry carrying a consignment of omega 3 capsules has overturned due to the high winds..

A spokesperson said the driver will be fine. He's just suffered a few super fish oil injuries.

●●●●●●●●●●●●

I just saw a sports car, driven by a scantily-clad young sheep.

It was in a lamb bikini

●●●●●●●●●●●●

I used to date an air stewardess from Helsinki.

I dropped her off at work one day and she just vanished into Finnair.

●●●●●●●●●●●●

Presents and birthdays

For my birthday I got a book about how they fix ships together.

It's riveting.

⁎⁎⁎⁎⁎⁎⁎⁎⁎⁎⁎⁎⁎

What is the best present?

A broken drum – you can't beat it.

⁎⁎⁎⁎⁎⁎⁎⁎⁎⁎⁎⁎⁎

.I wanted to buy my brother some camouflage trousers for his birthday.

I couldn't find any.

⁎⁎⁎⁎⁎⁎⁎⁎⁎⁎⁎⁎⁎

My parents gave me a huge ball of clay this year.

I don't know what to make of it.

⁎⁎⁎⁎⁎⁎⁎⁎⁎⁎⁎⁎⁎

What did the pirate say when he turned 80?

Aye Matey.

⁎⁎⁎⁎⁎⁎⁎⁎⁎⁎⁎⁎⁎

Professions

Why did the can-crusher quit his job?

Because it was soda pressing.

What did the farmer use to repair his shirt?

A cabbage patch.

Did you hear about the woman who got the job as a human cannonball?

She was fired.

What is an archaeologist?

Someone whose career is in ruins.

Did you hear about the mechanic who went to sleep under the leaky, old car?

He wanted to get up oily in the morning.

Who can shave six times a day and still have a beard?

A barber.

I just got hired at a company that makes bicycle wheels.

I'm the spokes-person.

Got a new job at the guillotine factory.

I'll beheading there shortly.

Our local chiropodist has been arrested as he keeps stealing small pieces of nail after treating patients.

He's a clipped toe maniac.

Applied for a job in a colliery but was turned down.

Never mined.

My dad always used to say "The first rule of theatre is to always leave them wanting more".

Great bloke.

Terrible anaesthetist.

* * *

I just turned down a job delivering for my local fruit and veg shop.

They offered to pay me in vegetables, but the celery was unacceptable.

* * *

I went through a terrible time in my life when I had a job as a theatre usher.

I was in a dark place back then.

* * *

An electrician arrives home at 3am.

His wife asks him, "Wire you insulate?"

He replies, "Watt's it to you? I'm Ohm, aren't I?"

* * *

I applied for a job as a carpenter the other day.

I had to demonstrate my skill with a piece of wood.

I nailed it.

I start my new job as an apprentice bell ringer later this morning.

It's my first day, so they'll just be showing me the ropes.

Someone once asked me who I'd most like to be trapped in a lift with.

I said, "a lift engineer".

Just been fired from my job as an interrogator.

I suppose I should have asked why.

In the monastery there was a brother whose job was to fry chips.

He was the chip monk.

My job is digging holes to look for water.

It is, well, boring.

I have a corner office with views of the entire city, drive a $500,000 vehicle, and that I'm paid to travel.

Yep, I'm a bus driver.

What is a web developer's favourite tea?

URL Grey.

⸺⸺⸺

What is an electricians favourite type of news?

Current events.

⸺⸺⸺

What kind of award did the dentist receive?

A little plaque.

⸺⸺⸺

Jack was a lumberjack who cut down 24 360 trees in his career and never lost count.

He kept a log of every one.

⸺⸺⸺

How do you become a professor?

Be degrees.

⸺⸺⸺

Why did the plumber lose his job?

It went down the drain.

⸺⸺⸺

How do undertakers talk?

In a grave manner.

⸺⸺⸺

What did the painter say to the wall?

One more crack like that and I'll plaster you.

Why are bakers silly?

They sell what they knead.

Why are train drivers anxious?

Their jobs are always on the line.

What kind of jokes do chiropodists like best?

Corny ones.

Pub

A man walked into a pub.
Ouch.

---

f(x)=2x3 walks into a bar.
The barman says,
'Sorry, we don't cater for functions'

Times New Roman, Arial, and Sans Serif walk into a bar.
Before they can order a drink the bartender yells.
"Get out, we don't serve your type here!"

I've done a survey on how people walk home from the pub.
The results are staggering.

The worst pub I've ever been in was called The Fiddle.

It was a vile inn.

⁎⁂⁂⁂⁂⁂⁂⁂⁂⁂⁎

Three men walked into a bar.

The fourth ducked.

⁎⁂⁂⁂⁂⁂⁂⁂⁂⁂⁎

Bacon and eggs walk into a bar.

The bartender says: "Sorry we don't serve breakfast."

⁎⁂⁂⁂⁂⁂⁂⁂⁂⁂⁎

A Priest, Iman and Rabbit walk into a café.

The rabbit says, "I'm sorry, I think I'm a typo."

⁎⁂⁂⁂⁂⁂⁂⁂⁂⁂⁎

Retail

A sweater I purchased was picking up static electricity, so I returned it to the store.

They gave me another one free of charge.

⁎⁕⁕⁕⁕⁕⁕⁕⁕⁕⁕⁕⁎

A man tried to sell me a coffin today.

I said: "That's the last thing I need."

⁎⁕⁕⁕⁕⁕⁕⁕⁕⁕⁕⁕⁎

Someone just tried to charge me £100 for some protein powder.

I thought "That's whey overpriced".

⁎⁕⁕⁕⁕⁕⁕⁕⁕⁕⁕⁕⁎

I went into the newsagents and asked the guy for a Twirl and a Boost.

He span round and said "You look fantastic, have you lost weight ?"

⁎⁕⁕⁕⁕⁕⁕⁕⁕⁕⁕⁕⁎

I work at Tesco in the fabric softener aisle but I've just been moved to dairy.

I'm out of my comfort zone.

⁂

Sadly we've lost some of our local businesses recently.

The bra shop has gone bust, the watch-menders has called time, the paper shop folded, the shoe repairers has been soled, the food blender factory gone into liquidation, and the TV aerial shop called in the receivers.

⁂

I'm confused, Amazon have delivered a load of Plasticine to me which I didn't order.

I don't know what to make of it?

⁂

How much does a chimney cost?

Nothing - it's on the house.

⁂

Bought a new shrub trimmer today! I proudly it showed my friend.

I said, "It's cutting hedge technology!"

⁂

Anyone want to buy a broken barometer?

No pressure.

⁂

My friend just hired a limo for £1000 but it didn't come with a driver.

Imagine spending all that money with nothing to chauffeur it.

⁕⁕⁕⁕⁕⁕⁕⁕⁕⁕⁕⁕⁕

I didn't realize the reopening of the Lego store was going to be so popular...

People were lining up for blocks.

⁕⁕⁕⁕⁕⁕⁕⁕⁕⁕⁕⁕⁕

I was in the supermarket when this guy threw a block of Cheddar at me.

Outraged, I shouted: "Well, that's not very mature, is it?"

⁕⁕⁕⁕⁕⁕⁕⁕⁕⁕⁕⁕⁕

I went into a pet shop and asked for twelve bees. The shopkeeper counted out thirteen and handed them over.

"You've given me one too many."

"That one is a freebie."

⁕⁕⁕⁕⁕⁕⁕⁕⁕⁕⁕⁕⁕

Where's the best place in America to shop for a football kit?

New Jersey.

⁕⁕⁕⁕⁕⁕⁕⁕⁕⁕⁕⁕⁕

I went to the opticians yesterday.

Made a total spectacle of myself.

⁕⁕⁕⁕⁕⁕⁕⁕⁕⁕⁕⁕⁕

Riddles

What gets wetter the more it dries?

A towel.

What bow can't be tied?

A rainbow.

What can you serve but not eat?

A volleyball.

What can you hold without touching it?

Your breath.

When you look for something, why is it always in the last place you look?

Because when you find it, you stop looking.

・●●●●●●●●●●・

Which is faster, hot or cold?

Hot, you can catch a cold.

・●●●●●●●●●●・

How can a man go 8 days without sleep?

He only sleeps at night.

・●●●●●●●●●●・

What runs around a field without moving?

A fence.

・●●●●●●●●●●・

What do you get after it's been taken?

A photo.

・●●●●●●●●●●・

If everyone bought a white car, what would we have?

A white carnation.

・●●●●●●●●●●・

What can you make that can't be seen?

Noise.

・●●●●●●●●●●・

A man found an old coin and declared that the date on it was 150 B.C. This could not be true. Why?

Because B.C. is counting backwards from the birth of Christ. If Christ hadn't been born yet, there were no dates in B.C. yet.

∘●●●●●●●●●●●∘

Which is heavier, a pound of lead or a pound of feathers?

The same – a pound is a pound!

∘●●●●●●●●●●●∘

What has a head and a tail, but no body?

A coin.

∘●●●●●●●●●●●∘

I'm light as a feather, yet the strongest man can't hold me for more than 5 minutes. What am I?

Breath.

∘●●●●●●●●●●●∘

When is a door not a door?

When it's ajar.

∘●●●●●●●●●●●∘

What kind of cheese is made backwards?

Edam.

∘●●●●●●●●●●●∘

Jimmy's mother had three children. The first was named April, the next was named May. What was the name of the third child?

Jimmy of course!

⁂

What kind of coat can only be put on when wet?

A coat of paint.

⁂

What occurs once in a minute, twice in a moment, and never in one thousand years?

The letter M.

⁂

What runs, but never walks, often murmurs – never talks, has a bed but never sleeps, has a mouth but never eats?

A river.

⁂

If you are running in a race and you pass the person in second place, what place are you in?

Second place.

⁂

What gets sharper the more you use it?

Your brain.

⁂

If I have it, I don't share it. If I share it, I don't have it. What is it?

A secret.

What can you catch but not throw?

A cold.

How many months have 28 days?

All 12 months.

They come out at night without being called, and are lost in the day without being stolen. What are they?

Stars.

What is full of holes but can still hold water?

A sponge.

Two in front, two in behind, and one in the middle. How many are there?

Three.   (1 2) 3   1 (2 3) 1 (2) 3

What begins with an 'e,' ends with an 'e' but only has one letter?

An envelope.

Why is an old-fashioned radio like roast pork?

They both have lots of crackling.

⁂

If the red house is made of red bricks and the brown house is made of brown bricks, what is a green house made of?

Glass.

⁂

What's the longest word?

Smiles – there's a mile between the first and last letter.

⁂

Which building always has the most stories?

A library.

⁂

What do polar bears and plumbers have in common?

They both want a good seal.

⁂

What is made of leather, a foot long and sounds like a sneeze?

A shoe.

School Jokes

What was the dog awarded after he left university?

A pedigree

What's the fruitiest subject at school?

History – it's full of dates.

Why did the teacher wear sunglasses?

His class was so bright.

Did you hear about the cross-eyed teacher?

She couldn't control her pupils.

What do we do with crude oil?

Teach it good manners.

Why did the school cook get a shock?

He stepped on a teacake and a currant went up his leg.

Why was the broom late for school?

It overswept.

Why did the teacher put the lights on?

The class was so dim.

Which word do students always spell incorrectly?

Incorrectly.

Why did one pencil tell the other pencil it looked old and worn out?

Because it was blunt.

Why did the teacher jump into the swimming pool?

She wanted to test the water.

Where does success come before work?

In the dictionary.

What's a cow's favourite lesson?

Moo-sic.

What schoolbag is always tired?

A knapsack.

Student: Are "well" and "actually" both single-syllable words?

Teacher: well yes, but actually no.

I'm trying to learn the alphabet but I can't get past X.

I don't know why.

Know what's remarkable?

Whiteboards.

The robber waved a gun and warned the bank teller: "Fill up this bag with cash or else you're geography!"

"You mean history?" "Don't change the subject!"

I was thinking of doing Hisory in uni
But I couldn't see any future in it.

⁃⁂⁂⁂⁂⁂⁂⁂⁂⁂⁃

Did you hear about the excellent geography teacher?
They had abroad knowledge of the subject.

⁃⁂⁂⁂⁂⁂⁂⁂⁂⁂⁃

Science Jokes

Two atoms are walking down the street.

One atom says to the other, "I think I have lost an electron."

The other says, "Are you sure?"

"Yes, I'm positive."

A photon checks into a hotel and the receptionist asks "Would you like some help with your luggage?"

The photon replies, "No thanks, I'm travelling light."

Sodium sodium sodium sodium sodium sodium sodium sodium Batman!

What is a physicist's favourite food?

Fission chips.

●●●●●●●●●●●●

Why did Erwin Schrödinger, Paul Dirac and Wolfgang Pauli work in very small garages?

Because they were quantum mechanics.

●●●●●●●●●●●●

They have just found the gene for shyness. They would have found it earlier, but it was hiding behind two other genes.

●●●●●●●●●●●●

A statistician is someone who tells you, when you've got your head in the fridge and your feet in the oven, that you're – on average - very comfortable.

●●●●●●●●●●●●

There are 10 kinds of people in this world, those who understand binary, and those who don't.

●●●●●●●●●●●●

A chemistry teacher is recruited as a radio operator in the first world war. He soon becomes familiar with the military habit of abbreviating everything. As his unit comes under sustained attack, he is asked to urgently inform his HQ. "NaCl over NaOH! NaCl over NaOH!" he says. "NaCl over NaOH?" shouts his officer. "What do you mean?" "The base is under a salt!" came the reply.

●●●●●●●●●●●●

Which animal dissolves faster in a lake: a brown bear or a white bear?

The white bear - it's more polar.

∙∙∙∙∙∙∙∙∙∙∙∙∙

What do you call a tube with a degree?

A graduated cylinder

∙∙∙∙∙∙∙∙∙∙∙∙∙

Albert Einstein finished joint-first in a rap contest last night.

Apparently E equals MC Squared.

∙∙∙∙∙∙∙∙∙∙∙∙∙

Why was the scarecrow so happy?

Cause he was outstanding in his field.

∙∙∙∙∙∙∙∙∙∙∙∙∙

I thought growing my own lettuce would be difficult but it was quite easy in the end.

It's not rocket science.

∙∙∙∙∙∙∙∙∙∙∙∙∙

My Physics teacher says my understanding of forces is the worst he's ever known.

I think he's pushing my leg.

∙∙∙∙∙∙∙∙∙∙∙∙∙

The programmer's wife tells him: "Run to the store and pick up a loaf of bread. If they have eggs, get a dozen."

The programmer comes home with 12 loaves of bread.

⁕⁕⁕⁕⁕⁕⁕⁕⁕⁕⁕⁕⁕

Asked to monitor an alpha particle generator, Dr. Jones replied, "I'll keep an ion it"

⁕⁕⁕⁕⁕⁕⁕⁕⁕⁕⁕⁕⁕

How do you know if a plant is politically persecuted for not transporting water and other nutrients? It requests a xylem.

⁕⁕⁕⁕⁕⁕⁕⁕⁕⁕⁕⁕⁕

That damn Higgs Boson. Always thinking the world revolves around him.

He's got a bit of a God complex.

⁕⁕⁕⁕⁕⁕⁕⁕⁕⁕⁕⁕⁕

What do you do with a dead chemist?

Barium!

⁕⁕⁕⁕⁕⁕⁕⁕⁕⁕⁕⁕⁕

Man walks into a chemist.

"Hey, have you got any Adenine Triphosphate."

"That'll be 80p."

⁕⁕⁕⁕⁕⁕⁕⁕⁕⁕⁕⁕⁕

I'd tell you a good chemistry joke, but all the good ones argon.

⁕⁕⁕⁕⁕⁕⁕⁕⁕⁕⁕⁕

Did you hear about the man who got cooled to absolute zero?

He's 0K now.

⁕⁕⁕⁕⁕⁕⁕⁕⁕⁕⁕⁕

What did the Greek chemist synthesise when he added sodium formate to his favourite dish? HCOONa moussaka.

⁕⁕⁕⁕⁕⁕⁕⁕⁕⁕⁕⁕

Which Bond villain manufactured acid rain?

Dr NO.

⁕⁕⁕⁕⁕⁕⁕⁕⁕⁕⁕⁕

Where do we get mercury from?

HG Wells.

⁕⁕⁕⁕⁕⁕⁕⁕⁕⁕⁕⁕

What is the name of the first electricity detective?

Sherlock Ohms.

I'll get me coat.

⁕⁕⁕⁕⁕⁕⁕⁕⁕⁕⁕⁕

What do they pay the policeman on night shift?

Copper nitrate.

A neutron walks into bar, orders a beer and drinks it. "What do I owe you?"

The bartender answers, "For you, no charge."

※※※※※※※※※※※

If you're not part of the solution, you're part of the precipitate.

※※※※※※※※※※※

What do you do with a sick chemist?

Well If you can't helium, and you can't curium, then you might as well barium.

※※※※※※※※※※※

What happened to the man who was stopped for having sodium chloride and a nine-volt in his car?

He was booked for a salt and battery.

※※※※※※※※※※※

Why can't you trust atoms?

They make up everything.

※※※※※※※※※※※

A Higgs Boson goes into a church. The priest runs up and says "you can't come in here!" "Why not?" says the Higgs Boson "without me, there is no mass".

※※※※※※※※※※※

Remember math and alcohol do not mix!

Do not drink and derive!

※※※※※※※※※※※

What do you call a ring of Fe+2 ions?

A ferrous wheel.

What do you call a tooth placed in a litre of water?

A one molar solution.

A gold bar walks into a bar, the barman says, "A u, get out of here".

What did the alkane say to the alkene?

It takes alkynes to make a world!

How many molecules in a bowl of guacamole?

Avacado's number.

Why is your nose in the middle of your face?

Because it's the scenter.

Where do bad rainbows go?

Prism.

The pulley is the most egotistical of all machines.

It's always the centre of a tension.

* * * * * * * * * * * *

If I don't perfect human cloning...

I won't be able to live with myself.

* * * * * * * * * * * *

What do you call a participation trophy in astronomy?

A constellation prize.

* * * * * * * * * * * *

What's heavier a gallon of water of a gallon of butane?

Water because butane is a lighter fuel.

* * * * * * * * * * * *

"Dad, can you tell me what a solar eclipse is?"

No sun.

* * * * * * * * * * * *

I caught my son chewing on electrical cords.

So I had to ground him. He's doing better currently, and is now conducting himself properly.

* * * * * * * * * * * *

What do you get when you mix sulfur, tungsten and silver?

SWAg.

* * * * * * * * * * * *

How do sulfur and oxygen communicate?

A sulfone.

What do you call iron blowing in the wind?

Febreze.

Why did the acid go to the gym?

To become a buffer solution.

Why does hamburger have lower energy than steak?

Because it's in the ground state.

Why did carbon marry hydrogen?

They bonded well from the moment they met.

A Physicist went out with a Biologist

But there was no Chemistry.

What do dipoles say in passing?

Do you have a moment?

What would you call a clown in jail?

Silicon (silly con).

What weapon can you make from potassium, nickel and iron?

A KNiFe.

Why are Chemists great at solving problems?

They have all the solutions.

Anyone know any jokes about sodium?

Na.

What is a cation afraid of?

A dogion.

What kind of ghosts haunt chemistry facilities?

Methylated spirits.

According to a chemist, why is the world so diverse?

It is made up of alkynes of people.

The name's Bond. Ionic Bond. Taken, not shared.

What did the flower say after it told a joke?

I was just pollen your leg.

What did the big flower say to the little flower?

What's up bud.

What do sad fir trees do?

Pine.

What did one earthquake say to the other earthquake?

It's not my fault.

Why did the germ cross the microscope?

To get to the other slide.

What happens if you get a gigabyte?

It megahertz.

What did one cloud say to the other cloud?

I'm cirrus about you.

When a plant is sad what do other plants do?

Photosympathise.

What do you call an acid with attitude?

A-mean-oh acid.

Skeleton Jokes

Why couldn't the skeleton laugh?

He lost his funny bone.

Why did the skeleton go to the barbeque?

To get a spare rib.

Why didn't the skeleton go to the ball?

He had no body to go with.

What did the femur say to the patella?

I kneed you.

Why did the skeleton cross the road?

To get to the Body Shop.

Why was the skeleton a coward?

He had no guts.

Space

What did the astronaut say when the spaceship took a wrong turn?

I didn't planet this way.

How do you put a baby astronaut to sleep?

You rocket.

Why was the astronaut eating a sandwich as his spaceship took off?

It was launch time.

Why didn't the astronaut land on the moon?

It was full.

What kind of music do planets sing?

Neptunes.

What do aliens like to read?

Comet books.

What did one lightning bolt say to the other lightening bolt?

You're shocking.

Star Wars

My sword doesn't weigh much.

It's my light saber.

What kind of car does a Jedi drive?

A Toy-Yoda.

My son Luke loves that we named our children after Star Wars characters.

My daughter Chewbacca not so much.

What did Yoda say when he saw himself on Blu-ray for the first time?

'HDMI.'

Why did the movies come out 4, 5, 6, 1, 2, 3?
In charge of scheduling, Yoda was.

⁎⁎⁎⁎⁎⁎⁎⁎⁎⁎⁎⁎

How warm is it inside a tauntaun?
Lukewarm.

⁎⁎⁎⁎⁎⁎⁎⁎⁎⁎⁎⁎

Luke had Wookie steak for dinner.
He said it was a little chewy.

⁎⁎⁎⁎⁎⁎⁎⁎⁎⁎⁎⁎

Is BB hungry?
No BB8.

⁎⁎⁎⁎⁎⁎⁎⁎⁎⁎⁎⁎

What do you need to reroute droids?
R2-Detour.

⁎⁎⁎⁎⁎⁎⁎⁎⁎⁎⁎⁎

What do you call five Siths piled on top of a lightsaber?
A sith-kebab.

⁎⁎⁎⁎⁎⁎⁎⁎⁎⁎⁎⁎

Which program do Jedi use to open PDF files?
Adobe Wan Kenobi.

⁎⁎⁎⁎⁎⁎⁎⁎⁎⁎⁎⁎

Which website did Chewbacca create to share Empire secrets?

Wookieleaks.

⁕❀❀❀❀❀❀❀❀❀❀⁕

How is Duct tape like the Force?

It has a Dark Side, a Light side and it binds the galaxy together.

⁕❀❀❀❀❀❀❀❀❀❀⁕

Where do Gungans store their things?

In Jar-Jars.

⁕❀❀❀❀❀❀❀❀❀❀⁕

Why did Anakin Skywalker cross the road?

To get to the Dark Side.

⁕❀❀❀❀❀❀❀❀❀❀⁕

Why is Yoda such a good gardener?

He has green fingers.

⁕❀❀❀❀❀❀❀❀❀❀⁕

What did Obi-Wan tell Luke when his young apprentice was having a difficult time using chopsticks at the Chinese restaurant?

"Use the forks, Luke."

⁕❀❀❀❀❀❀❀❀❀❀⁕

What's a Jawa's favourite pasta?

Rotini.

⁎⁎⁎⁎⁎⁎⁎⁎⁎⁎⁎⁎⁎

Why can't you count on Yoda to pick up a bar tab?

He's always a little short.

⁎⁎⁎⁎⁎⁎⁎⁎⁎⁎⁎⁎⁎

Why is a Jedi knight never lonely?

Because the force is always with him.

⁎⁎⁎⁎⁎⁎⁎⁎⁎⁎⁎⁎⁎

How do you get down from a Bantha?

You don't. You get down from a goose.

⁎⁎⁎⁎⁎⁎⁎⁎⁎⁎⁎⁎⁎

What do you call it when only one Star Wars character gives you some help?

A Hand Solo.

⁎⁎⁎⁎⁎⁎⁎⁎⁎⁎⁎⁎⁎

How do you unlock doors on Kashyyyk?

With a woo-key.

⁎⁎⁎⁎⁎⁎⁎⁎⁎⁎⁎⁎⁎

What do you call Chewbacca when he got bits of chocolate stuck in his fur?

A chocolate chip Wookie.

⁎⁎⁎⁎⁎⁎⁎⁎⁎⁎⁎⁎⁎

How did Darth Vader know what Luke was getting for his birthday?

He felt his presents.

⁂

Who tries to be a Jedi?

Obi-Wannabe.

⁂

Which Jedi became a rock star?

Bon Jovi-Wan Kenobi.

"I'm worried about your little sister, goin' 'bout town going out wearing that shiny suit."

"It's just a Phas'ma."

⁂

Why couldn't Princess Leia find love?

She was looking in all Alderaan places.

⁂

How many sith does it take to screw in a lightbulb?

None, they love the dark side.

⁂

What do you call a droid that takes the long way around?

R2 detour

Time

What happened to the clock that fell into the sheep dip?

It lost all its ticks.

Why was the clock feeling sick?

It was run down.

I recently received a book with "do not read until the year 2030" written on the cover.

But that's a story for another time.

Can February March?

No, but April May.

Last Thursday my son was moping around and I told him, if you think Thursdays are sad, just wait two more days. He asked why?

Because it'll be sadder day.

The worst thing about eating a clock?

Passing the time.

Technology

Look out for a new email scam about the warranty on your small kitchen appliances expiring.

It's a completely different kettle of phish.

※※※※※※※※※※※

A large oil company has announced that it is going to start producing fuel from insect urine.

I think it's BP.

※※※※※※※※※※※

I got an e-mail saying Google Earth can now read maps backwards

I thought, that's just spam

※※※※※※※※※※※

I met a bloke from Australia who said he works on IT systems.

I said "Do you come from a LAN down under?"

⁂

The internet connection in my farm is really sketchy, so I moved the modem to the barn.

Now I have stable wifi.

⁂

My friend claims that he can print a gun using his 3D printer, but I'm not impressed.

I've had a Canon printer for years.

⁂

Spiders are the only web developers who love finding bugs.

⁂

Water

How does the ocean say hello?

It waves!

How do you cut a wave in half?

Use a sea saw.

What washes up on tiny beaches?

Microwaves!

What happened when the boat carrying blue paint hit the boat carrying red paint?

All of the passengers were marooned.

What's black, incredibly rude and floats on water?

Crude oil.

Why did the crab blush?

Because the seaweed.

What do you find in the middle of the ocean?

The letter 'e'.

What's the best way to communicate with a fish?

Drop him a line.

What did the blue what say when he collided with the bottlenose dolphin?

I didn't do it on porpoise.

What are the strongest creature in the ocean.

Mussels.

Where do very young fish go to every morning?

Plaice school.

What's the laziest fish in the world?

A kipper.

Why do fish swim in salt water?

Pepper would make them sneeze.

Where do you weigh a whale?

At a whale-weigh station.

What's the best way to catch a fish?

Get someone to throw it to you.

What do you call?

What do you call an airline passenger covered in salt and pepper?

A seasoned traveller.

What do you call a deer with no eyes?

No idea.

What do you call a deer with no eyes and no legs?

Still no idea.

What do you call a dog who loves to have their hair washed?

A shampoodle.

What do you call a giraffe with three legs?
Eileen.

What do you call a camel with three humps?
Humphrey.

What do you call an overeducated plumber?
A drain surgeon.

What do you call a tree with a croaky voice?
A hoarse chestnut.

What do you call a man with a car on his head?
Jack.

What do you call a man with a seagull on his head?
Cliff.

What do you call a man with a spade on his head?
Doug.

What to you call a man without a spade on his head?
Douglas.

What do you call a man with turf on his head?
Pete.

What do you call a man who floats in the ocean?
Bob.

What do you call a woman who catches lots of fish?
Annette.

What do you call a woman with a frog on her head?
Lily.

What do you call a woman on the beach?
Sandy.

What do you call a man at the doorstep?
Matt.

What do you call a man with sports equipment on his head?

Jim.

⁎⦿⦿⦿⦿⁎⦿⦿⦿⦿⁎

What to you call a woman with a toilet on her head?

Lou.

⁎⦿⦿⦿⦿⁎⦿⦿⦿⦿⁎

What do you call a woman with two toilets on her head?

Lulu.

⁎⦿⦿⦿⦿⁎⦿⦿⦿⦿⁎

What do you call a man with a rabbit up his jumper?

Warren.

⁎⦿⦿⦿⦿⁎⦿⦿⦿⦿⁎

What do you call a man who can't stand up?

Neale.

⁎⦿⦿⦿⦿⁎⦿⦿⦿⦿⁎

What do you call a skeleton that can't be bothered to get out of bed?

Lazy bones.

What do you call a lady who works in an orchard?

Pip.

●●●●●●●●●●●●●

What do you call a magician who has lost their magic?

Ian.

●●●●●●●●●●●●●

What do you call a man who pours a lot of drinks?

Phil.

●●●●●●●●●●●●●

What do you call a knight who is afraid to fight?

Sir Render.

●●●●●●●●●●●●●

What do you call a Knight who is no longer needed?

Sir Plus.

●●●●●●●●●●●●●

What do you call a man with gravy, meat and potatoes on his head?

Stu.

●●●●●●●●●●●●●

What do you call a man in a pile of leaves?

Russell.

●●●●●●●●●●●●●

What do you call a woman with a cash register on her head?

Tilly.

What do you call a woman with a tortoise on her head?

Shelley.

What do you call a man who likes to dunk biscuits in his tea?

Duncan.

What do you call a girl with the surname Curtain?

I hope it's not Annette?

No it's Velvet.

What do you get if you cross?

What do you get if you cross a sheep and a kangaroo?

A woolly jumper.

What do you get if you cross a grizzly bear and a harp?

A bear-faced lyre.

What do you get if you cross a sweet potato and a jazz musician?

A yam session.

What do you get when you cross a snowman with a vampire?

Frostbite.

What do you get if you cross an apple with a shellfish?

A crab apple

What do you get if you cross a dog with a daisy?

A colli-flower.

What do you get when you cross a cat and a lemon?

A sour puss.

What do you get if you cross Father Christmas with a duck?

A Christmas quacker.

What do you get if you cross a thought with a lightbulb?

A bright idea.

What do you get when you cross elephants with a fish?

Swimming trunks.

What do you get if you cross a chicken with a cow?

Roost beef.

What do you get if you cross a frog with a dog?

A croaker spaniel.

What do you get if you cross an elephant with a mouse?

Huge holes in the skirting boards.

What do you get if you cross a dog with an elephant?

A really nervous postman.

What do you get if you cross a comedian with an orange?

Peels of laughter.

What would you get if you crossed a vampire and a teacher?

Lots of blood tests.

What do you call it when you mix alcohol and American Literature?

Tequila Mockingbird.

What do you get if you cross a dog with a telephone?

A golden receiver.

Winter Jokes

What did one snowman say to the other snowman?

Can you smell carrots?

What do you call a snowman in Summer?

A puddle.

How do snowmen greet each other?

It's ice to meet you.

What does a bald snowman need?

An ice cap.

Why did the snowman sit on the marshmallow?
Because he didn't want to fall in the hot chocolate.

What do you sing at a snowman's birthday party?
Freeze a jolly good fellow.

What do snowmen do at weekends?
Just chill out.

How do snowmen get around?
By icicle.

How can you tell if a snowman is angry with you?
He gives you a cold shoulder.

How do I build a shelter with ice?
I-gloo it together.

What's an ig?
An igloo with no toilet.

What do snowmen and snow women have?

Chill-dren

How do you make your own antifreeze?

Send her to Antarctica.

What does an octopus wear in winter?

A coat of arms.

Words

The motivational speaker stood up on stage and said, "Litres, pints, gallons!"

That spoke volumes.

The word 'Diputseromneve' may look ridiculous.

But backwards it's even more stupid.

I was going through a really tough time. My friend came to me and said, "Bargain."

I replied, "Thanks, that means a great deal."

Why is nostalgia like grammar?

We find the present tense and the past perfect.

The guy who invented the umbrella was going to call it the brella.

But he hesitated.

⸺⸺⸺

My friend asked me what procrastinate means.

I said: "I'll tell you later."

⸺⸺⸺

What do you say to comfort a grammar nazi?

"There, their, they're."

⸺⸺⸺

I have a pen that can write underwater.

It can also write other words too.

⸺⸺⸺

I'm friends with 25 letters of the alphabet.

I don't know y.

⸺⸺⸺

What starts with a W and ends with a T.

It really does.

⸺⸺⸺

Printed in Great Britain
by Amazon